The Unsearchable Riches of Christ

Chosen to be Sons of God

Bill Vincent

The Unsearchable Riches of Christ

Copyright © 2015 by Bill Vincent. All rights reserved.

No part of this publication may be reproduced, stored in a retrieval system or transmitted in any way by any means, electronic, mechanical, photocopy, recording or otherwise without the prior permission of the author except as provided by USA copyright law.

Published By
Revival Waves of Glory Books & Publishing
PO Box 596
Litchfield, IL 62056
http://www.revivalwavesofgloryministries.com

Revival Waves of Glory Books & Publishing is committed to excellence in the publishing industry.

Published in the United States of America

eBook: 978-1-312-64392-5

Paperback: 978-0692534496

Table of Contents

CHAPTER ONE **UNSEARCHABLE RICHES OF CHRIST** 7

CHAPTER TWO **THINK LIKE SONS OF GOD** 11

CHAPTER THREE **REDEMPTION** 17

CHAPTER FOUR **RESURRECTION POWER** 23

CHAPTER FIVE **ADOPTED SONS OF GOD** 27

CHAPTER SIX **ENEMIES OF REVIVAL** 39

CHAPTER SEVEN **REVELATION OF GRACE** 47

CHAPTER EIGHT **COMMUNION WITH CHRIST** 51

CHAPTER NINE **THE PURPOSE OF REVIVAL** 59

CHAPTER TEN **REDEMPTION OF THE TIMES** 63

CHAPTER ELEVEN **FULL PENTECOST** 83

CHAPTER TWELVE **POSITION TO RECEIVE** 87

CHAPTER THIRTEEN **THE EL SHADDAI BLESSING!** 91

ABOUT THE AUTHOR 97

RECOMMENDED BOOKS 99

Chapter One
Unsearchable Riches of Christ

There is no way we can ever discover all the riches of the Lord's richness. For over a week I've been thinking about this verse: "Unto me, who am less than the least of all saints, is this grace given, that I should preach among the Gentiles the *unsearchable riches of Christ*" (Ephesians 3:8 KJV).

The unsearchable, unending, unlimited, and mysterious riches of Christ. This is truly the beauty of mystery. I love the word "mystery"-it means secret. It implies that we get the honor to search the heart of God for revelation. This verse and these thoughts are truly making me hunger for more.

> Proverbs 25:2 *It is* the glory of God to conceal a thing: but the honour of kings *is* to search out a matter.

Of course, this mystery of the endless treasures of who and what we are refer to the mystery of the Gospel. Imagine the full wealth and knowledge of the cross. Grace will never end. It makes me hunger and long to know more. Who can fully comprehend that He is mindful of us? We are born again (renewed) and blessed with every spiritual blessing in Christ. Think about the glory of the resurrection-walking with God and miracles. These are some of the great mysteries of the gospel, and there are many more.

You could study for all of eternity on the beauty, mystery, power, mercy, and majesty of the cross and it would not be enough! It is unsearchable! At the same time, we have the Mind of Christ. What is even more amazing is that God wants to share His mysteries, even secrets of the universe, with us. This is the purpose of intimacy and fellowship with His Spirit. We have the Spirit of wisdom and revelation dwelling inside of us to reveal the truths of the Gospel! Wow!!

> Amos 3:7 Surely the Lord GOD will do nothing, but he revealeth his secret unto his servants the prophets.

One of the greatest mysteries is "Christ in you, the hope of glory" (Colossians 1:27).

Another great mystery revealed in Christ and the Father are "hidden all the treasures of wisdom and knowledge" (Colossians 2:3).

I love this thought about the mystery of godliness or to be God-in likeness.

> 1 Timothy 3:16 And without controversy great is the mystery of godliness: God was manifest in the flesh, justified in the Spirit, seen of angels, preached unto the Gentiles, believed on in the world, received up into glory.

I love the true key to godliness-it is God manifested in our flesh. When we surrender fully to the Holy Spirit, He will manifest Jesus in us and we will have His likeness (Godliness).

Unsearchable Riches of Christ

> Ephesians 3:6 That the Gentiles should be fellowheirs, and of the same body, and partakers of his promise in Christ by the gospel:

I think the greatest gift of the Holy Spirit is found in this promise in the gospel of Matthew.

> Matthew 13:11 He answered and said unto them, Because it is given unto you to know the mysteries of the kingdom of heaven, but to them it is not given.

That means we can know the "mystery of His will" (Ephesians 1:9,11). We make the mystery of His kingdom known. We can also know and search out the mystery of the resurrection (I Corinthians 15:51). There is a beauty in searching and discovering the unsearchable riches of Christ.

In all of our preaching the glorious mysteries and riches of Christ, let us remember the glory of the cross

Chapter Two
Think Like Sons of God

When we find ourselves as Sons of God it reveals privileges we would never find any other way. Whether we are men or women, we are all to think like sons of God.

> 1 John 3:1, 2 Behold, what manner of love the Father hath bestowed upon us, that we should be called the sons of God: therefore the world knoweth us not, because it knew him not. Beloved, now are we the sons of God, and it doth not yet appear what we shall be: but we know that, when he shall appear, we shall be like him; for we shall see him as he is.

What a high relationship is that of a Son, and what privileges it brings! What care and tenderness the son expects from his Father, and what love the Father feels towards the Son.

In fulfillment of Christ's prayer, "I have declared unto them Thy name, and will declare it: that the love wherewith Thou hast loved Me may be in them" (John 17:26 KJV). Take a look at this powerful quote, "The Spirit is given to His redeemed to signify the sameness of the Father's love unto His Son and unto His sons. Thus, the inhabitation of the Spirit in the Christian is both the surest sign of God's fatherly love and the proof of his adoption."

Think Like Sons of God

We need to think like sons. We are joint heirs with Christ. Because we are sons, we have the Spirit of His Son assuring us of our salvation and royal inheritance (Galatians 4:6-7).

Think about being a Son, which means to occupy a place in God's family in which He loves us just as much as He loves His only begotten Son. It means we have a place in God's family just as eternal and secure as His only begotten Son.

Before we can fully understand our rights and privileges as an adopted Sons and Daughters of God, let's take a look again at what true adoption was in Roman times when Paul used the word.

Under Roman law a child could not possess anything, and any inheritance willed to him or a gift given to him became the property of the father. So it was a serious step to take a child out of one family and put him another. The ritual of adoption must have been very impressive.

Twice, the real father "sold" his son, and twice he bought him back. Finally, he sold him a third time and at the third sale, he did not buy him back. After this, the adopting father had to go one of the principal Roman magistrates, and plead the case for the adoption. And only after all this had been gone through was the adoption complete. But when the adoption was complete, it was complete indeed. The person who had been adopted had all the rights of a legitimate son in his new family and completely lost all rights in his old family. Furthermore, all of his old debts were considered paid-he was a new person.

Think Like Sons of God

We don't live like peasants when we know His love. A child of the kingdom does not live as a slave of the world. We now respond to God in love as a Father, not a Master. We want to be like Him because He loves us, not out of fear of judgment. We are friends of God, not servants.

Our motive for ministry as Sons is never selfish-ambition, competition, and pride. A Son has the nature of his Father, a servant and slave do not. Servants have no future and obey out of fear not love. Sons are rich and servants are poor. Sons have fathers where servants have masters. God calls us friends.

> Joh 15:15 Henceforth I call you not servants; for the servant knoweth not what his lord doeth: but I have called you friends; for all things that I have heard of my Father I have made known unto you.

Sonship means we move out of the resting assurance that our Father is pleased with us. A true revelation of the idea of spiritual adoption is that God chose, purchased, and predestined us in His love to be a Son. This is the key to being accepted and secure in our identity. We are Sons.

A servant doesn't know his Master's will and has to be told what to do. He relates to God on the basis of what he does. If he does well, he thinks God loves him more. Someone who thinks like a slave will take liberty from serving. A Son finds liberty in serving. A Son relates to God on the basis of the Father's love first shown to him (see 1 John 4:19). A servant waits on God. A Son does what he sees his Father doing (John 5:19).

The Bible goes on to say,

> Joh 5:20 For the Father loveth the Son, and sheweth him all things that himself doeth: and he will shew him greater works than these, that ye may marvel.

A servant does not know what his Master is doing, but friendship and intimacy is key to seeing what the Father does. A revelation of the depth of the Father's love is key to receiving revelation of His purpose and will. We do the works of the Father as Sons, not because we have to but because we want to. As true Sons of the Father, we must be able to say to the world, "Watch my life. Listen to what I say. See the works I do. It's all about my Father."

We see clearly from the Gospel of John that Jesus was moved by His intimacy with the Father. If we wish to understand what motivated and guided Jesus day by day, then we must examine the intimate relationship He had with our heavenly Father. We too can think and act like sons.

> John 5:19 Then answered Jesus and said unto them, Verily, verily, I say unto you, The Son can do nothing of himself, but what he seeth the Father do: for what things soever he doeth, these also doeth the Son likewise.
>
> John 5:30 I can of mine own self do nothing: as I hear, I judge: and my judgment is just; because I seek not mine own will, but the will of the Father which hath sent me.
>
> John 7:16 Jesus answered them, and said, My doctrine is not mine, but his that sent me.
>
> John 8:16 And yet if I judge, my judgment is true: for I am not alone, but I and the Father that sent me.

John 8:26 I have many things to say and to judge of you: but he that sent me is true; and I speak to the world those things which I have heard of him.

Joh, 8:28, 29 Then said Jesus unto them, When ye have lifted up the Son of man, then shall ye know that I am *he,* and *that* I do nothing of myself; but as my Father hath taught me, I speak these things. And he that sent me is with me: the Father hath not left me alone; for I do always those things that please him.

John 8:38 I speak that which I have seen with my Father: and ye do that which ye have seen with your father.

John 8:40 But now ye seek to kill me, a man that hath told you the truth, which I have heard of God: this did not Abraham.

John 12:49, 50 For I have not spoken of myself; but the Father which sent me, he gave me a commandment, what I should say, and what I should speak. And I know that his commandment is life everlasting: whatsoever I speak therefore, even as the Father said unto me, so I speak.

John 14:10 Believest thou not that I am in the Father, and the Father in me? the words that I speak unto you I speak not of myself: but the Father that dwelleth in me, he doeth the works.

John 14:24 He that loveth me not keepeth not my sayings: and the word which ye hear is not mine, but the Father's which sent me.

Jesus was operating out of a close, intimate relationship with the Father. The words He spoke, the miracles He performed, and the places He went were not random, but were ordained by heaven.

Look at the last phrase of Romans 8:17:

> Romans 8:17 And if children, then heirs; heirs of God, and joint-heirs with Christ; if so be that we suffer with *him*, that we may be also glorified together.

God is making us mature Sons. Sonship is properly speaking the pinnacle of human nature and the full expression of the image of God, with which we have been endowed. Jesus, as the Son of the Father, is thus truly and fully what a human being was created to be. Our Sonship will be nothing other than full conformity to His image!

Chapter Three
Redemption

Recently God has revealed many of the false teachings of grace. The thing I'm most concerned about is that the Body of Christ won't receive the true Grace that God has provided through His Son's death and resurrection. The false grace that I was referring to is the belief that our salvation doesn't come with true repentance. The belief that we are once saved always saved with no need of repentance ever again. This is a lie and true Sons of God, should know this. I think as Christians we know that we are saved by grace. We sometimes forget the power in the simple truths of the Gospel. We miss out on the power that's available through the cross. It will truly come alive in your life again when you remember what Jesus accomplished. I for one am falling in love again with Jesus as I study afresh the glories of Calvary in a new way. Today we look at redemption!

Look at this quote: "The heart of the gospel is redemption, and the essence of redemption is the substitutionary sacrifice of Christ." -Spurgeon

> Ephesians 1:7   In whom we have redemption through his blood, the forgiveness of sins, according to the riches of his grace;

We have been redeemed (purchased our freedom out of slavery; to buy one out) because of the shed blood of Jesus. The blood also gives us forgiveness and cleansing of sin. I want you to think about this verse. One, we have redemption.

Redemption

And two, we have forgiveness. These are similar but two different things. It all happened because of the shed blood of Jesus because His grace is rich.

So let's look at the glory of redemption. The word implies so much more than forgiveness or salvation-it means to be delivered from, rescued, or brought back from slavery. The purpose of being redeemed is that you can have freedom from judgment, and the consequences of sin and death. It is so you can enjoy being brought back from captivity to liberty.

Redemption is the act of buying something back, or paying a price to return something to your possession. We know that the blood of Jesus was the purchase price for us to be redeemed from sin and all its power, which included sickness, disease, death, and poverty. The slave was not just purchased from the dock of slavery, but the word means to go from one thing to another thing.

> Colossians 1:13, 14 Who hath delivered us from the power of darkness, and hath translated *us* into the kingdom of his dear Son: In whom we have redemption through his blood, *even* the forgiveness of sins:

Truly, I am a possession of God; blood bought and have passed from death to life.

It was by His redemption that we have free grace to be justified in His sight.

> 2 Corinthians 5:21 For he hath made him *to be* sin for us, who knew no sin; that we might be made the righteousness of God in him.

Redemption

> Romans 3:23, 24 For all have sinned, and come short of the glory of God; Being justified freely by his grace through the redemption that is in Christ Jesus:

I love that Jesus not only spoke of His death to the disciples on a cross, but He spoke of His purpose. Christ Jesus "gave His life a ransom (payment) for many" (Matthew 20:28). And by that ransom He worked for us a great redemption. How great a price He paid.

When talking about the fruit of redemption, redemption is the legal access or identification (what we are in Christ) or to our being in Christ. It is sealed and eternal (Hebrews 9:11-12). Here are some of the legal benefits of our redemption.

The blood deals with what we have done, whereas the cross (redemption) deals with what we are. Here is what Watchman of the Lord need,

1. Redemption is our claim to the righteousness of Christ. We stand before God right, with no sense of guilt, shame, or fear, and without any condemnation or sin consciousness.

2. We are redeemed from the curse of the law. We are made now to receive the blessings of Abraham.

3. "By your blood you ransomed people for God from every tribe and language and people and nation, and you have made them a kingdom and priests" (Revelation 5:9-10 ESV).

4. I think one of the greatest benefits of redemption is that I am not my own-I am bought at a price (1 Corinthians 6:19). I am now adopted into His family.

Redemption

5. Healing through the redemption and covenant that was made in blood was a part of the blessing of the cross. It was a part of being redeemed from the curse of the law. It must be preached as the full message of the cross.

Jesus bore our sickness and disease at the same time that He bore in His body our sins.

> Matthew 8:16, 17 When the even was come, they brought unto him many that were possessed with devils: and he cast out the spirits with *his* word, and healed all that were sick: That it might be fulfilled which was spoken by Esaias the prophet, saying, Himself took our infirmities, and bare *our* sicknesses.

He healed all that were sick. The word "infirmity" in this passage here means: disease, weakness, frailty, or sickness. In addition, the word here for "He took our infirmities" means "to lay hold of or to take in order to carry away, to claim for one's self.

> Isaiah 53:4, 5 Surely he hath borne our griefs, and carried our sorrows: yet we did esteem him stricken, smitten of God, and afflicted. But he *was* wounded for our transgressions, *he was* bruised for our iniquities: the chastisement of our peace *was* upon him; and with his stripes we are healed.

He "bore" in Hebrew means, "to take away one's sorrow and grief (pain). In Hebrew this word implies "sickness, disease, and pain, both physical and soul." The word for "sorrow" means, "to have physical and mental pain." The word "healed" (ropha) in the Hebrew means, "to make one healthful or to cure." It can also suggest a gradual process. The word used for "stripes" in this verse means "to bruise." Jesus bore our sickness, pain, sorrow, and disease at the same time

Redemption

He bore our sins in His body on a tree (the cross). "By his wounds (stripes) you have been healed" (I Peter 2:24 NIV).

To have redemption is to have been forgiven, be righteous, have peace, have the Holy Spirit, reconciliation, freedom, adoption, be holy and justified. These are just a few blessings of redemption. The final act of redemption will be our bodies (Romans 8:23).

Remember how precious this gift of redemption is.

> 1 Peter 1:18, 19 Forasmuch as ye know that ye were not redeemed with corruptible things, *as* silver and gold, from your vain conversation *received* by tradition from your fathers; But with the precious blood of Christ, as of a lamb without blemish and without spot:

Redemption

Chapter Four
Resurrection Power

This topic is more for today than many believers will ever admit. We need to tap into the power that is available through the resurrection of Jesus Christ. This Chapter will help you understand resurrection power and walk in victory over sin, sickness, disease, death, and poverty. This is key to victorious living.

> Romans 6:3, 4 Know ye not, that so many of us as were baptized into Jesus Christ were baptized into his death? Therefore we are buried with him by baptism into death: that like as Christ was raised up from the dead by the glory of the Father, even so we also should walk in newness of life.

I started developing a resurrection mindset, not just the future resurrection but in my thinking now. There will be an ultimate resurrection and glorification. There is a resurrection power working in us now. My spirit has been raised from the dead already (Romans 6:3). I know what it's like; it is like that same "glory" that raised Christ from the dead. That same glory is what has touched our spirits and made us alive.

> Romans 8:11 But if the Spirit of him that raised up Jesus from the dead dwell in you, he that raised up Christ from the dead shall also quicken your mortal bodies by his Spirit that dwelleth in you.

Resurrection Power

> Romans 6:5 For if we have been planted together in the likeness of his death, we shall be also *in the likeness* of *his* resurrection:

I've already experienced the very same resurrection power that raised Jesus from the dead. It not only has touched me, it's working inside of me! "For this purpose also I labor, striving according to His power, which mightily works within me" (Colossians 1:29 NASB). That revelation is like being gloriously born again, again!

> Romans 5:17 For if by one man's offence death reigned by one; much more they which receive abundance of grace and of the gift of righteousness shall reign in life by one, Jesus Christ.)

We are reigning in life as kings through resurrection and the grace of God. Sin and death have no dominion over me. "Knowing that Christ, having been raised from the dead, dies no more. Death no longer has dominion over Him" (Romans 6:9 NKJV). This means that sickness, poverty, and disease have no dominion over me because I have died and been resurrected to share in His likeness.

"The law of the spirit of life in Christ Jesus has made me free from the law of sin and death" (Romans 8:2). There is a new law of grace. The law of sin, death, and condemnation was a spiritual law of death and bondage. All of hell was ready to back-up and enforce that law. But the new law of the Spirit of life, the law of grace in Christ Jesus, has made me free from the law of sin and death. Now all of heaven and His angels are ready to enforce this law! Therefore, the truth is that grace says that I'm not sick (sickness can be defeated)! I am blessed. I'm free and no longer under death's curse of sin, sickness, disease, and poverty. It's a spiritual law of grace and freedom. "Devil, you can't hold me down!" There is a new law of the Spirit realm-the law of the Spirit of life in Christ Jesus. "There is therefore now no condemnation to those who are in Christ Jesus" (Romans 8:1 NKJV). There is no guilt, punishment, sentence, or shame.

> Romans 6:10, 11 For in that he died, he died unto sin once: but in that he liveth, he liveth unto God. Likewise reckon ye also yourselves to be dead indeed unto sin, but alive unto God through Jesus Christ our Lord.

You are no longer a natural being that has a spirit; you're a spiritual being that has a body! You're a brand new creation in Christ who lives, for a time, on the earth-one who is learning to live in your true nature, in Christ Jesus, which is Spirit (2 Corinthians 5:17).

I believe God is going to bring the body of Christ together in unity, positioned to receive a corporate revelation concerning the truth. "It is no longer I who live, but Christ who lives in me" (Galatians 2:20 NKJV). We need to be possessed by the Holy Spirit in such a way that we know it's no longer us who lives, but Christ who lives in us. We'll be walking in this reality when Jesus actually lives through us like He wants to-through our eyes, ears, words, touch, and presence.

I'm talking about the likeness of His resurrection (Romans 6:5) and the idea that as we walk in "newness of life," we walk in victory. You cannot tell me that there is resurrection power operating in your life if you're being defeated in sin. (Sin shall have no dominion over you.) That resurrection power is yours if you'll use it! It is the work of the Holy Spirit in us. He is called the Spirit of holiness. "And who through the Spirit of holiness was appointed the Son of God in power, by his resurrection from the dead" (Romans 1:4 NIV). He is also the Spirit of resurrection, and only He can help overcome what the flesh wants. He responds when we seek holiness by grace and demonstrate reverential fear of the Lord

Actually, the Spirit of holiness works in seven ways. The Holy Spirit corrects, counsels, strengthens, helps, intercedes, is our defense attorney, and the comforter called alongside. It's the Holy Spirit residing within us, and the effective working of His power working within us, that makes us holy, sanctifies us, and makes us righteous.

Two keys to this are His grace and our obedience-in love. In fact, we can only manifest God's kingdom to the extent we're willing to sacrifice, surrender, and be obedient to His will. The greater the obedience and total surrender, the greater the manifestation of power.

Chapter Five
Adopted Sons of God

One of the most powerful revelations I ever heard was through the late Myles Munroe. He spoke that when we were adopted as Sons, we became Ambassadors of Heaven. The understanding of adoption as sons and daughters is key to the ministry of the Holy Spirit. Apart from the Holy Spirit, we can never have the assurance that we are children of God. "For all who are being led by the Spirit of God, these are sons of God" (Romans 8:14). The true heart of a child of the Father says, "I can do nothing of myself" (John 5:19). Sons and daughters are moved by the revelation of God's love and grace. Their service is an overflow of gratitude and submission. Their dependence is on the Holy Spirit because as a child they seek to do His will. Jesus said, "I only do the things I see My Father doing" (John 5:19). When we are led by the Spirit, our desire will be for His will to be done. We will live to bring honor to His name.

Our English word adoption is filled with the ideas of love, grace, compassion, and intimate relationship. In the ancient world, the adopted person lost all rights in his old family, gained all the rights of a fully legitimate son in his new family, and in the most literal sense, and in the most binding legal way, he got a new father. In addition, all his debts were legally canceled. His old life was completely erased and he was regarded by the law as a new person. Similarly, in spiritual adoption, the moment undeserving sinners are adopted by their heavenly Father as His children, their entire status is eternally changed-they receive a new name, a new family, new rights, and new expectations. Unlike human adoption, they also receive a new nature, actually becoming partakers of the divine nature!

Adoption is to be brought into relationship with the Father in a manner that bestows us the full rights of Sonship and full paternal intimacy. We need to understand that we were enslaved to another "father" (Satan) by virtue of our sin and guilt, and thus needed to be redeemed so we could legally belong to our true Father. I think understanding Paul's thinking in the culture in which he wrote about adoption is key to grasping the full awesomeness of being sons and daughters.

> Romans 8:15, 16 For ye have not received the spirit of bondage again to fear; but ye have received the Spirit of adoption, whereby we cry, Abba, Father. The Spirit itself beareth witness with our spirit, that we are the children of God:

The Holy Spirit teaches us to be sons and daughters and how to relate to God as Father. We now have the "spirit of adoption." The primary ministry of the Holy Spirit is to teach us that we are accepted, secure, chosen, and desired by God. Even though He had no duty to, in His generous grace He chose us.

The Holy Spirit is bearing witness to our spirits that we are now sons and daughters. It is an intimate parental cry to say "Abba" (Daddy). We have no fear because in the revelation of the Father's love, there is no fear. Perfect love casts out fear. We have no fear because we have Sonship and confidence that He is leading, teaching, and assuring us of our inheritance in the family. We now bear His name upon us. "And if children, then heirs; heirs of God, and joint-heirs with Christ; if so be that we suffer with him, that we may be also glorified together" (Romans 8:17, KJV). The Holy Spirit is the seal and guarantee of our redemption, and the promise that we have a future glory and resurrection. He is the comfort and embrace that strengthens us in all suffering.

> Ephesians 1:4 According as he hath chosen us in him before the foundation of the world, that we should be holy and without blame before him in love:

So adoption was part of God's plan before we were even born. He chose us in Him before the foundation of the world that we should be holy and blameless before Him. In love He predestined us for adoption through Jesus Christ, according to the purpose of His will, to the praise of His glorious grace (Ephesians 1:4-6). God chose me for the purpose of Sonship so that I would be a co-heir. All of this was because of His grace. Our adoption (Sonship) is not based on our being worthy or attractive. It is based on the free, sovereign grace of God, conceived in God's heart before the world even began and purchased for us by the blood of Jesus.

I love the idea of adoption. Many scholars and other interpretations of this passage of Scripture suggest the word adoption is actually Sonship. There is some difference in Sonship versus adoption. For example, Martin Luther in his day believed stronger in the word Sonship because it suggests we have the very life of God in us. It's more than being adopted with someone else's nature. We are now partakers of the divine nature of God (2 Peter 1:4). "I have been crucified with Christ; and it is no longer I who live, but Christ lives in me; and the life which I now live in the flesh I live by faith in the Son of God, who loved me and gave Himself up for me" (Galatians 2:20). Luther believed Sonship was the stronger thinking of Paul's use of the word in Roman times, because through being born again, we now have a new nature and the Holy Spirit dwells in us.

Sonship is union with Christ that comes from our having been begotten of God to be His children in life and nature by virtue of the divine birth. It qualifies us to receive the position and right of sons and daughters in our union with the Son in the Father by the Holy Spirit.

We need to think and relate to God as children and not servants. Jesus always thought of Himself as a Son. He referred to us as family-brothers and sisters. God does not deal with us as master, servant, and slave but friends. "Henceforth I call you not servants; for the servant knoweth not what his lord doeth, but I have called you friends" (John 15:15 KJV). The intimacy and fellowship we see with Jesus and the Father is key to our knowing Him in an intimate way.

> John 14:23 Jesus answered and said unto him, If a man love me, he will keep my words: and my Father will love him, and we will come unto him, and make our abode with him.

Jesus was the one that introduced us to the imagery of being with Him in "the Father's house." Think of the atmosphere of a healthy home with the warmth, peace, joy, and security of being in a family loved unconditionally. This is what it means to be a son or daughter of God.

Adopted Sons of God

In the Lord's Prayer, Our Father, Abba Father, God as Father, is always accessible. His heart is generous-He knows the things we have need of before we ask Him (Matthew 6:7-8). The Father's care and providence is part of this relationship as sons and daughters. Jesus said, "Do not be worried about your life, as to what you will eat or what you will drink; nor for your body, as to what you will put on" (Matthew 6:25). We must have total trust in our Father's care. "If you then, being evil, know how to give good gifts to your children, how much more will your Father who is in heaven give what is good to those that ask Him" (Matthew 7:11). Being a son or daughter and knowing the Father loves us is only part of the revelation. We need to learn how to be sons and daughters of God. We need to value God's care and provision as Father, but be sure that we have intimacy, love, and relationship with Him more than what He can do for us. Our question today needs to be, "How can I be a son or daughter in this family, God?"

> John 16:27 For the Father himself loveth you, because ye have loved me, and have believed that I came out from God.

We need to understand that knowing the Father means we must have His affection and embrace. It is only the love of God that can satisfy the thirsty heart. We want to hear Him say, "Well done, good and faithful servant." We want His presence and the safety of dwelling in His arms.

The prayer that Jesus prayed in John 17:23 that they would know You love them, Father, as You have loved Me" is the same love of Jesus. In being a son and a father, I had many great as well as bad experiences. A father cannot just be a father in name and position. He must be a present and active father to his sons and daughters. Earthy fathers try to always provide well. In all of that, still the generosity of our Father in heaven is limitless.

Those fathers who care and provide for their family still need to be near to their sons. We still need to learn to give and receive affection. It can be something the Holy Spirit gives and teaches us.

We are accepted and precious in His sight. "But the very hairs of your head are all numbered" (Matthew 10:30). Just knowing the truth of this verse gives us security, comfort, and rest.

> Zephaniah 3:17 The LORD thy God in the midst of thee *is* mighty; he will save, he will rejoice over thee with joy; he will rest in his love, he will joy over thee with singing.

Jesus said, "Just as the Father has loved Me, I have also loved you" (John 15:9). Jesus loves me for who I am, not what I do. He loves me in the same way the Father loves Him. Just some of these verses reveal God's value in us. It gives us our sense of belonging and security. It is an amazing thought that when the Father looks at Jesus, He sees and loves us with the same love.

> Ephesians 3:17-19 That Christ may dwell in your hearts by faith; that ye, being rooted and grounded in love, May be able to comprehend with all saints what *is* the breadth, and length, and depth, and height; And to know the love of Christ, which passeth knowledge, that ye might be filled with all the fulness of God.

We need to understand that knowing the Father means we must have His affection and embrace. It is only the love of

Adopted Sons of God

God that can satisfy the thirsty heart. We want to hear Him say, "Well done, good and faithful servant." We want His presence and the safety of dwelling in His arms.

It's an amazing thought that as adopted sons and daughters of our heavenly Father, we are full heirs and co-heirs along with His own unique Son, Jesus Christ.

> 1 John 5:4 For whatsoever is born of God overcometh the world: and this is the victory that overcometh the world, *even* our faith.

"The people who are given this power or right or authority to become sons of God are in an entirely different category from others who do not believe. These are those who believe in His name, and the adoption only happens to them, not to the others. Similarly in Romans 8:15, Paul is addressing only believers, those who are 'in Christ' and who have been given the 'Spirit of Christ' (Romans 8:9). Our Lord put it like this to the unbelieving Jews who had said that they were all children of God: 'If God were your Father,' He said, 'ye would love Me' (John 8:42). Then He was more specific and said, 'Ye are of your father the devil, and the more than enough to demonstrate the case that not all men and women are the children of God in this special sense.' Our Lord Himself draws that sharp distinction. And the Apostle Paul in the epistle to the Ephesians says that we were all 'by nature the children of wrath, even as others' (Ephesians 2:3). And it is only those who have been quickened with Christ who have become the children of God.

Spiritual adoption gives us placement, privilege, and rights as sons and daughters. Regeneration gives us new nature as sons and daughters. My adoption is a bestowal of intimate relationship. My regeneration is the transformation of my old nature. Our nature is an overcoming one. We have a victorious and strong Spirit. We are born of His divine nature, and are created in His likeness and image. What an amazing thought! Not just His likeness or image in physical features, but in Spirit and nature. We represent the Father, what He did, who He is, and how He acts. Our image is now Christ. "Because as He is, so also are we in this world" (I John 4:17). This Sonship is not just a title or privilege; it is of nature. We possess the very life of God. This Sonship is our right, life, position, and inheritance through our intimacy with the Father. We now have the responsibility as sons and daughters of God to re-present the Father to the world.

"That which is born of the flesh is flesh; and that which is born of the Spirit is spirit" (John 3:6). I am Spirit in a body. We are born by the way of the Holy Spirit and now led by the Spirit. Like the wind that blows wherever it wishes, so are those born of the Spirit. God is Spirit. We are created by nature in His likeness now. We are Spirit in our capacities. We touch, taste, smell, hear, and feel like God. We now have a new heart and Spirit, and are being transformed in the renewing of our minds so we can think, feel, and act like Christ.

> Galatians 4:5 To redeem them that were under the law, that we might receive the adoption of sons.

The adopted status of believers means that in and through Christ we know the Father loves us as He loves His Son and will share with us all the glory that is Christ's (see Romans 8:17, 38-39). We now bear His character, presence, and power, and are no longer slaves but sons and daughters. We are in His family and He is our Father. True Sonship is an inner cry of the heart to know our Father (Abba, Daddy) and an acceptance that we are His. The spirit of adoption bears witness to our spirits that we are sons and daughters. Apart from the work of the Holy Spirit, we will never experience the Father's love or have confidence that we are children. Our home, inheritance, and estate are in the Father's house.

> John 1:12 But as many as received him, to them gave he power to become the sons of God, *even* to them that believe on his name:

In the regeneration (born again), we become children. Regeneration is the key to our transformation. In adoption, God gives us relationship as sons and daughters. We must grow in the Lord's grace to become mature sons and daughters in Christ. Mature sons and daughters carry the fullness of God. "Until we all attain to the unity of the faith, and of the knowledge of the Son of God, to a mature man, to the measure of the stature which belongs to the fullness of Christ" (Ephesians 4:13).

As children, we are heirs of God and co-heirs with the inheritance of Christ. What He possesses, we now possess. The adoption tells us that the sum and substance of our promised inheritance is a share in the glory of Christ (Romans 8:17). In the ancient world, adoption implies the loss of all old things in a family, but now as legitimate children, we get all the blessing of our new family.

I like the idea of adoption because it means God wants and choses me. Sonship (adoption) gives the assurance, security, and confidence that the Father's (parental) providence, protection, and care are ours because we are in His family. This intimacy will produce servants not slaves. In a family, we do things out of love, not duty. Relationship cannot be lost, even if fellowship is broken. He is our Father by blood (Jesus) and His commitment remains to us, even when we fail. Repentance restores fellowship. It's an amazing thought that as adopted sons an daughters of our heavenly Father, we are full heirs and co-heirs along with His own unique Son, Jesus Christ.

> Ephesians 1:5 Having predestinated us unto the adoption of children by Jesus Christ to himself, according to the good pleasure of his will,

God's glory is not just in us and to us, but through us because those whom He has called, He has justified and those He has justified, He has glorified (Romans 8:30). "But we have this treasure (glory) in earthen vessels" (2 Corinthians 4:7). How much of a capacity do we have as mere men to receive and manifest the glory of God? I'm inspired to think of Moses' face shining and Peter's shadow healing as a great start. We need to be hungry for more.

When the body of Christ has a deeper revelation of what it really means to carry the glory presence of God, they will be filled with so much of the fullness (full measure) of God that they will release His glory through prayers, actions, and worship filling the very atmosphere with the knowledge of the glory of the Lord and be a full expression of Him in the earth.

> Romans 8:19 For the earnest expectation of the creature waiteth for the manifestation of the sons of God.

When we see the manifestation and the revealing of the sons and daughters of God, who understand who they are and what they have, they will take responsibility to defeat sin (corruption, sickness, disease, death, poverty) and bring the glory of God with them wherever they go. Because of the glorious liberty of the children of God, believers will carry the revelation of who they are and what they have in Christ, and they will be releasers of glory.

Instead of looking at how defeated the world is, let's look at the potential there is for the world to become like the kingdom of God under His rule. We can truly help to establish His reign. "The kingdoms of this world have become the kingdoms of our Lord, and of his Christ, and he shall reign for ever and ever" (Revelation 11:15, KJV). We need to understand that it's the knowledge of the glory of the Lord released through us as sons and daughters of God that will cause His kingdom to come on earth as it is in heaven.

> Romans 8:21 Because the creature itself also shall be delivered from the bondage of corruption into the glorious liberty of the children of God.

I do believe that light is greater than darkness. I also believe there will be an ultimate redemption of the body and glorification in the final resurrection (verse 18). However, I also believe we have a greater capacity now to manifest heaven on earth and be light in the darkness. We must come into our place of glory dominion. We set captives free and bring the world into His joy and freedom. Our liberty is glorious.

> Isaiah 60:1, 2 Arise, shine; for thy light is come, and the glory of the LORD is risen upon thee. For, behold, the darkness shall cover the earth, and gross darkness the people: but the LORD shall arise upon thee, and his glory shall be seen upon thee.

Adopted Sons of God

The glory will be greater in darkness. The light of His glorious gospel will shine through. We will be burning ones that carry the fire and torch of revival to the nations. I believe that God revealing His sons and daughters in this hour is in the message of Sonship, adoption, and understanding who we are, or better yet who Christ is in us. In spiritual adoption, the moment undeserving sinners are adopted by their heavenly Father as His sons and daughters, their entire status is eternally changed-they receive a new name, a new family, new rights, and new expectations. However, unlike human adoption, they also receive a new nature, actually becoming partakers of the divine nature!

Chapter Six
Enemies of Revival

When we see true revival happen, it changes us forever. One of the most important things is to expose and remove the enemies of Revival. I believe this prophetic message and teaching will truly help you be free in a greater way and encounter the grace of God as well as overcome the greatest enemies that oppose revival today.

The only true key to overcoming a religious (law) and political spirit is grace. These spirits are two of the greatest enemies of revival today. The answer to revival is grace. It empowers us to live free and victoriously. The beauty of grace is truly irresistible. Once you taste it, nothing will satisfy except more grace. Grace is Jesus! A fresh revelation of the grace of God will humble us and help us overcome the pride of a political spirit. This will help us walk in the true heart of kingdom culture and release true revival.

Jesus always spoke of three different leavens. They were religious, political, and the leaven of the kingdom (grace). "And he charged them, saying, Take heed, beware of the leaven of the Pharisees, and of the leaven of Herod" (Mark 8:15 KJV).

The religious spirit is anything that says "I must do something in my own strength to please God or my own attempt to become like Him." It will hold on to that which is familiar and comfortable rather than moving on from glory to glory. The law is dead religion, and it always puts rules and laws above relationship and intimacy. A political spirit is more concerned about appearance and protecting the message. The political spirit says, "I must do something to please others and at all costs maintain my position!" It is more concerned about what others may think if we associate with someone or something that may be perceived as negative than be concerned with true love. The political and religious spirits (law) work closely together to oppose true grace and revival.

The political spirit is man's attempt to please others. The political spirit's agenda is always to rally men, preferably leaders, around a message of perceived correctness and to protect that message. A political spirit is more concerned about a perceived rightness and association. It works through fear and concerns itself with what people think rather than showing the heart of Jesus. When presented an opportunity to fellowship with certain members of the body of Christ, the political spirit asks what will people think if it associates with them. It is more concerned about protecting a false appearance and message rather than kingdom unity. A political spirit will attempt to secure its position no matter what. It is truly rooted in the fear of man, alliances with money, prestige, and power. One true key to overcoming a political spirit is the government of God and living with a kingdom message letting the rule and reign of the Spirit in our hearts.

These spirits are willing to compromise all that one holds dear for the sake of gaining and maintaining power through the political and religious systems at any cost! The political spirit appeals to our lust for power and fame. It is rooted in the pride of man and is what Satan offered Jesus. The political spirit is an attempt by man to elevate himself and create of a platform of the highest power and influence.

The only true key to overcoming a religious (law) spirit and walking in freedom is true grace. It empowers us to live free and victoriously. A fresh revelation of the grace of God will humble us and help us overcome the pride of a political spirit and walk in the true heart of a kingdom culture.

People think that because they go to a church that is religious, that makes them religious by association. We tend to think that if something or someone, especially a leader, is religious then everyone in the church is religious. I believe that we can walk in freedom in any place that we are in. Jesus was in the same places that the Pharisees and Sadducees were. He was able to go into their churches and synagogues and be around the people without Himself becoming bound by the spirit of religion.

> John 8:31-37 Then said Jesus to those Jews which believed on him, If ye continue in my word, *then* are ye my disciples indeed; And ye shall know the truth, and the truth shall make you free. They answered him, We be Abraham's seed, and were never in bondage to any man: how sayest thou, Ye shall be made free? Jesus answered them, Verily, verily, I say unto you, Whosoever committeth sin is the servant of sin. And the servant abideth not in the house for ever: *but* the Son abideth ever. If the Son therefore shall make you free, ye shall be free indeed. I know

> that ye are Abraham's seed; but ye seek to kill me, because my word hath no place in you.

They sought to kill Jesus because they were bound by the religious spirit, and they were working under the power of the devil. But Jesus realized that they were in bondage. That is why He said to them, "You shall know the truth, and the truth shall make you free." Most people who are in this type of bondage do not know that they need to be set free. We should pray that they might see so that they might be set free. Jesus knew when the Sadducees came that they were looking to trap Him and ultimately slay Him. Realizing that they were bound by the religious spirit, He tried to reach them by bringing them into truth. He could have gotten an attitude with them and even exposed them and their motive publicly.

The religious spirit breeds fear and intimidation. To those who are not religious, religion can breed a rebellious attitude. Our automatic tendency when someone says, "you have to..." is to say, "I don't have to do anything, man. Forget that!" We are just as wrong as they are because of our attitude. We are responsible to react with character, grace, and integrity to a person bound by the religious spirit. When it looked like Jesus was dealing harshly with men who were religious, He always dealt with the spirit behind religion and not the person. That is why when Jesus was on the cross, put there by religious people, He asked the Father to forgive them for what they were doing.

We need to realize that we do not wrestle with men, churches, or ministries. We need to reach those that have not yet come into the grace. We are not better than them; we are just free. We should never use our freedom to cause unnecessary offenses. I love to dance before the Lord in worship. However, if I go into a church and the pastor asks for people to not dance, I will not. If I do, then it is not freedom but rebellion. I believe the only way to truly help people be free is grace. The way some people present God today creates an impression that His mercy only lasts for a moment, but His anger lasts forever. Mercy triumphs over judgment.

Much of what we do as Christians begins with fiery passion and a drive from the Holy Spirit. Then it becomes an obligation and duty that we perform because we know it is what we are "supposed" to do rather than by grace. Grace is the Holy Spirit's influence helping us deny ourselves so that we can receive everything that Christ gave us!

> Matthew 22:23-32 The same day came to him the Sadducees, which say that there is no resurrection, and asked him, Saying, Master, Moses said, If a man die, having no children, his brother shall marry his wife, and raise up seed unto his brother. Now there were with us seven brethren: and the first, when he had married a wife, deceased, and, having no issue, left his wife unto his brother: Likewise the second also, and the third, unto the seventh. And last of all the woman died also. Therefore in the resurrection whose wife shall she be of the seven? for they all had her. Jesus answered and said unto them, Ye do err, not knowing the scriptures, nor the power of God. For in the resurrection they neither marry, nor are given in marriage, but are as the angels of God in heaven. But as touching the resurrection of the dead, have ye not read that which was spoken unto you by God, saying, I am the God of Abraham, and the God of Isaac, and the God of Jacob? God is not the God of the dead, but of the living.

Religion keeps you in control. We like law because it tells us what to do externally and when we do it, our conscience feels a whole lot better. This takes the place of inner peace that comes from being in right relationship with God. With this religious mindset we feel like we are right with God, and yet it is the complete opposite of how Jesus walked. Though some of us are not as steeped in tradition like many religions, we still have rituals of our own that we do to make us feel better. In addition, through this process it loses the passion and becomes obligation.

The religious spirit (law) likes to keep us from the things of the Spirit. Under its influence, we often become so law-focused, or doctrinally obsessed, that we lose the passion for power and anything that involves feelings. We also can easily walk in law instead of love. When we become more determined to punish someone for not following the letter of the law than to love them and see human need, it might be a good sign that we are operating under the influence of this spirit. Many times when we are giving ourselves over to this judgmental heart, we ourselves are doing the same or worse things.

> Matthew 12:1-8 At that time Jesus went on the sabbath day through the corn; and his disciples were an hungred, and began to pluck the ears of corn, and to eat. But when the Pharisees saw *it*, they said unto him, Behold, thy disciples do that which is not lawful to do upon the sabbath day. But he said unto them, Have ye not read what David did, when he was an hungred, and they that were with him; How he entered into the house of God, and did eat the shewbread, which was not lawful for him to eat, neither for them which were with him, but only for the priests? Or have ye not read in the law, how that on the sabbath days the priests in the temple profane the sabbath, and are blameless? But I say unto you, That in this place is *one* greater than the temple. But if ye had known what *this* meaneth, I will have mercy, and not sacrifice, ye would not have

condemned the guiltless. For the Son of man is Lord even of the sabbath day.

The religious spirit has a voice. It speaks in this way, "You have to get up early in the morning and pray. You have to tithe. You have to bless your meal each time you eat, before you eat. You have to have a good outward appearance. You have to be at every prayer meeting." These are all things that I do or have done. However, I don't want to do anything because I feel I have to. We do so many things out of obligation and duty. It is called pretense or hypocrisy when we draw near to God with our lips, but our hearts are far from Him. There is nothing wrong with doing the outward things. Many of them were commanded in the Old Testament. However, none of them was commanded with the intention that obedience would take place based on duty rather than passion and thankfulness of heart that God gave man a way to be forgiven.

> Matthew 12:9-13 And when he was departed thence, he went into their synagogue: And, behold, there was a man which had *his* hand withered. And they asked him, saying, Is it lawful to heal on the sabbath days? that they might accuse him. And he said unto them, What man shall there be among you, that shall have one sheep, and if it fall into a pit on the sabbath day, will he not lay hold on it, and lift *it* out? How much then is a man better than a sheep? Wherefore it is lawful to do well on the sabbath days. Then saith he to the man, Stretch forth thine hand. And he stretched *it* forth; and it was restored whole, like as the other.

Nothing is more damaging than a religious spirit binding a life. By placing rules and expectations on people, especially unbelievers and new believers, it cuts them off from wanting anything to do with God. Many times we are more worried about what we are going to look like rather than the value of a person's soul. How quick we are to come against people's outward sins and forget about our own inward darkness. If we value the heart of God toward His people rather than our own judgmental opinions, we will seek to guide with a gentle heart those who are bound by religion into truth and grace. Grace is needed to do anything good! Grace empowers the believer to do His will and grace enables us to believe and be hungry so we can walk in freedom.

Chapter Seven

Revelation of Grace

God is pouring out His supernatural Grace. This will be like nothing anyone has experienced before. This is a now Word being released.

> Psalms 85:10 Mercy and truth are met together; righteousness and peace have kissed *each other*.

Mercy and truth (Jesus was full of grace and truth) have finally come together like two friends after a long separation. Our love for the truth and grace of God must come together with His mercy and love. They need to be joined again. When they do, it will produce true peace and righteousness. The imagery used in this Psalm for restoration, renewal, mercy, and grace for Israel is an intimate kiss. On one side of the road we have mercy and peace; on the other side truth demands righteousness. They have finally reconciled in grace. This kiss happened at the cross. Righteousness and peace are sealed with a kiss. Redemption is bound in blood red love. The cross of Jesus is where God's justice and mercy kiss. I love what this releases in the earth.

> Psalms 85:11 Truth shall spring out of the earth; and righteousness shall look down from heaven.

The promises (truth) that are unfulfilled and hidden like buried seeds will now spring up and yield a fruitful harvest.

Now that we have reconciled with a kiss to truth and received mercy, we can receive the righteousness (justice) of God.

I have been meditating on the grace of God. The Lord continues to speak to me about how mercy and grace kiss. Understanding that God's mercy is His love (compassion) towards us in not receiving the judgment we deserve. The grace of God (undeserved favor and goodness) is more than just the reason we have salvation, righteousness, and justification by faith alone. Grace is also a restraining power to overcome sin. The grace of God, not my own strength or merit, to resist sin and temptation is the enabling (restraining) power for me to not fall in the mud. When God withdraws His hand of grace, we are powerless to overcome sin.

I have been thinking about the prodigal son (Luke 15:11-32). The youngest son insisted on receiving his share of the estate and squandering his inheritance in wild living. He then found himself in the mud with pigs. When we decide and insist on our own rebellion, God simply withdraws His grace (power) and we fall in the mud. We need God to bestow grace upon us so we can walk holy.

What I love about this parable is the imagery of the mercy and grace of God that restores us in a moment when we say like the lost son: "I will set out and go back to my father and say to him: Father, I have sinned against heaven and against you" (Luke 15:18 NIV).

We see in this parable the Father's love, grace, mercy, and compassion. Even while the son was still a long way off, he ran to him and embraced him with a kiss. "But while he was still a long way off, his father saw him and was filled with compassion for him; he ran to his son, threw his arms around him and kissed him" (Luke 15:20 NIV). This is a true picture of when mercy and grace have kissed. The restoration to his inheritance and his place in the father's house was immediate. His restoration was a celebration (Luke 15:22). "But the father said to his servants, 'Quick! Bring the best robe and put it on him. Put a ring on his finger and sandals on his feet. Bring the fattened calf and kill it. Let's have a feast and celebrate. For this son of mine was dead and is alive again; he was lost and is found.' So they began to celebrate" (Luke 15:22-24 NIV).

"Therefore let us draw near with confidence to the throne of grace, so that we may receive mercy and find grace to help in time of need" (Hebrews 4:16). What a great promise. We are called to the throne of grace, not to the throne of law. I have access to His very throne of glory with confidence and joy. Nothing can separate me from constant access and fellowship with Him. It is a throne built on grace to find mercy. The throne of grace is the mercy seat, sprinkled in the precious blood of Jesus. It is not a throne of judgment and condemnation, but the manifest love and acceptance of God.

This is another great picture of where mercy and grace have kissed and come together so we can be reconciled (mercy-forgiven) to God and find power (grace) to overcome sin. "We may receive mercy and find grace to help in time of need" (Hebrews 4:16). Mercy is not receiving the judgment we deserve for our sin, and we find in mercy the grace (restraining power) so we don't fall in the mud again.

The beauty of grace is truly irresistible, abounding and overflowing. Once you taste it, nothing will satisfy but more. Grace is Jesus!

Revelation of Grace

Chapter Eight
Communion With Christ

More and more God is drawing His children to a deeper intimacy than ever before. Today is your day to find those places of intimacy that will change your life. This verse gives true hope, assurance, and peace. "According as he hath chosen us in him before the foundation of the world, that we should be holy and without blame before him in love" (Ephesians 1:4 KJV). God chose us and secured us by His blood, before the beginning of time, that we be holy and without blame (guiltless) abiding in His love. It's always been in His purpose that we are in His love. It is His purpose that we are in love and communion.

> 1 John 1:3 That which we have seen and heard declare we unto you, that ye also may have fellowship with us: and truly our fellowship *is* with the Father, and with his Son Jesus Christ.

Communion is a relationship of shared (or mutual) affection. To experience communion, there needs to be fellowship and communication, shared affections, response, delight, and satisfaction. It needs to be an active communion (union) and not just a state of passivity.

Communion With Christ

There is no love of the Father separate from Christ, as we cannot love the Father without Christ! The love of God is poured out through the Holy Spirit because of Christ's sacrifice. True communion (union) is rooted in abiding love. "And hope does not disappoint, because the love of God has been poured out within our hearts through the Holy Spirit who was given to us" (Romans 5:5).

In true communion, there is always two parts. It's a mutual communication. First, we are secure and abiding in the revelation of His love for us. Then we respond with our mutual love and affection for Him.

We cannot truly love Him unless He loves us first. "In this is love, not that we loved God, but that He loved us and sent His Son to be the propitiation for our sins" (I John 4:10). Again, we have full confidence is His love, because He chose us and loved us first. "But God demonstrates His own love toward us, in that while we were yet sinners, Christ died for us" (Romans 5:8). Our love for God is in response to His love.

Assurance of the love of God for us is key to unbroken fellowship. The security of His love is the very foundation in which we walk with God. How do we truly know we are in this fellowship with the Father? "If we say that we have fellowship (communion) with Him and yet walk in the darkness, we lie and do not practice the truth" (I John 1:6). "He who says, 'I know Him' (I have communion with Him), and keeps not His commandments, is a liar, and the truth is not in him" (I John 2:4 NKJV). The greatest mistake we make is to think our fellowship with the Father, without holiness and obedience, as a fruit of faith, grace, and love, can be achieved. To keep His commandments serves only to prove the false to

Communion With Christ

be liars. The love of the world and of the Father do not dwell together.

> Ephesians 2:18 For through him we both have access by one Spirit unto the Father.
>
> Revelations 1:4, 5 John to the seven churches which are in Asia: Grace *be* unto you, and peace, from him which is, and which was, and which is to come; and from the seven Spirits which are before his throne; And from Jesus Christ, *who is* the faithful witness, *and* the first begotten of the dead, and the prince of the kings of the earth. Unto him that loved us, and washed us from our sins in his own blood,

The seven Spirits before the throne is the Holy Spirit of God. We see here again that the three members of the Godhead (Trinity) are joined together working in this verse. All of them mentioned are distinguished in their communication of grace and peace unto the saints. Grace and peace be unto you, from the Father, faithful witness (Jesus) and seven Spirits of God. Again we see in Corinthians God's desire for us is to have communion with each one of the distinct persons of the Godhead.

> 2 Corithians 13:14 The grace of the Lord Jesus Christ, and the love of God, and the communion of the Holy Ghost, *be* with you all. Amen.

We see here again the three distinct persons of the Godhead. It is the "love of God" that Paul peculiarly assigns to the person of the Father.

We see the fellowship of the Spirit is mentioned with the grace of Christ (Calvary). It is through faith by grace alone that we are saved. The cross was a manifestation of the love of God in action. It is through the Holy Spirit alone now that we can have fellowship with Christ in grace and with the Father in love.

"And he who loves Me will be loved by My Father, and I will love him and manifest Myself to him" (John 14:21 NKJV). - "manifest Myself in all My grace, presence, beauty, glory, and loveliness; you will know Me as I am." The real communication of grace in Christ is found in sending the Holy Ghost to save us. Then to create in us a habitual abiding grace that empowers us daily in our hearts and life with favor.

The word "communion" in this verse is referred to in the Greek text as "koininia." Communion in this context means unity, a close association, fellowship, close bond, or a partnership. The underlying message is sharing. So Paul was saying, "May you experience and share the intimate bond, the closeness, the unity, the fellowship of the Holy Spirit, Father and Son. Paul infers there is something a whole lot deeper to the Holy Ghost here than just gifts and anointing. We can now know koininia with God.

I have a koininia relationship with the Holy Spirit. I dialogue with Him constantly. There is a bond that is so close I can't even describe it. We share, talk, ask questions of each other, and communicate openly. I ask Him questions and He gives me answers, and vice-versa. There is freedom in our fellowship. He's like a close buddy and accompanies me everywhere. I keep in step with Him (see Galatians 5:25). I don't have to wait for Him to come upon me or manifest in some way; I just know He's there.

Communion With Christ

Our communion with Jesus is greater. "Now, this is in GRACE. This is everywhere ascribed to him by the way of eminency (John 1:14). He dwelt among us, full of grace and truth; grace in the truth and substance of it. All that went before was but typical and in representation; in the truth and substance it comes only by Christ. Grace and truth came by Jesus Christ, verse 17; and of His fullness have all we received, and grace for grace, verse 16; - that is, we have communion with Him in grace; we receive from Him all manner of grace whatever; and therein have we fellowship with Him."-John Owen

There are many benefits of communion with the Lord. Some of these reminders will make you truly hungry for more. Remember the beauty of the Holy Spirit!

He is my friend, peace, and God-the fire and wind beneath my sail. Through His mighty power, we will prevail. He is my rain, my love from above-the fountains of the deep, and the restorer of my soul. He is the mighty witness power within. He is the Spirit of Christ, gifts, and graces.

> 1 John 2:20 But ye have an unction from the Holy One, and ye know all things.

> 1 John 2:27 But the anointing which ye have received of him abideth in you, and ye need not that any man teach you: but as the same anointing teacheth you of all things, and is truth, and is no lie, and even as it hath taught you, ye shall abide in him.

I love that He is my teacher, discerner-the one that leads and guides me in truth. He is the Spirit of wisdom and revelation-the one who quickens the living word and brings to remembrance all the words and works of Jesus. He teaches and reveals the mind of God, my counsel and understanding. He is abiding, adoption, knowledge, and the fear of the Lord. The Holy Spirit is my comfort, assurance, and joy.

"But God has revealed them to us by His Spirit. Now we have received, not the spirit of the world, but the Spirit who is from God, that we might know the things that have been freely given to us by God" (I Corinthians 2:10-12 NKJV). He sends us His Spirit as He promised to make known His mind unto His saints, and to lead them into all truth. And then the apostle concludes, "We have known the mind of Christ" (I Corinthians 2:12). There is nothing in the heart of Jesus where His friends are concerned that He does not reveal to them. All His love, goodwill, the secrets of His covenant, direction, and the mysteries of the gospel, are told to us. And all this is spoken in opposition to unbelievers, with whom He has no communion. These know nothing of the mind of Christ as they should. "The natural man receiveth not the things of the Spirit of God" (I Corinthians 2:14 KJV).

> Romans 8:26, 27 Likewise the Spirit also helpeth our infirmities: for we know not what we should pray for as we ought: but the Spirit itself maketh intercession for us with groanings which cannot be uttered. And he that searcheth the hearts knoweth what *is* the mind of the Spirit, because he maketh intercession for the saints according to *the will of* God.

The greatest privilege of communion is His abiding, dwelling, habitual presence. "The one who keeps His commandments abides in Him, and He in him. We know by this that He abides in us, by the Spirit whom He has given us" (I John 3:24). This is the true union of communion-we abide in Him and He in us by the Holy Spirit. He has made us a habitation.

Communion With Christ

Chapter Nine
The Purpose of Revival

Revival has truly been a life changer for me. Once you taste of the spirit of revival you will never be satisfied with anything else. The greater we understand how desperately we need to be revived & hunger for that Encounter the more grace we will receive to seek him!

We need to understand our need to Live Again!

Lets talk about the fruit of Revival! A true fruit of Revival is a desire to change, awakened hunger, and new passion for Jesus and his word!

Definition of Revival

1) Revival refers to a spiritual reawakening from a state of dormancy or stagnation in the life of a believer.

2) It is a extraordinary movement of the Holy Spirit producing extraordinary results.

3) Times of refreshing from the presence of the Lord." (Acts 3:19)

The greater we understand how desperately we need to be revived & hunger for that Encounter the more grace we will receive to seek him!

The Purpose of Revival

Revival begins with hunger (intense desire for him) the Holy Spirit always comes to the hungry.

This will make you Hungry!

The power of God seemed to shake the whole assembly. Towards the close of the sermon, the cries of the distressed arose almost as loud as his voice. After the congregation was dismissed the solemnity increased, till the greater part of the multitude seemed engaged in the most solemn manner. No person seemed to wish to go home- hunger and sleep seemed to affect nobody- eternal things were the vast concern. Here awakening and converting work was to be found in every part of the multitude; and even some things strangely and wonderfully new to me.

This is why we need the fire of revival!

Cause us to Rejoice in him.

(Ps 85 1-6 AMP) The fruit of Revival!!!

Revival will always bring a renewed praise & worship.

We need to pray, "Revive us to rejoice in You!"

> Habakkuk 3:2 O LORD, I have heard thy speech, *and* was afraid: O LORD, revive thy work in the midst of the years, in the midst of the years make known; in wrath remember mercy.

Quicken us to call on your name!

The Purpose of Revival

> Psalms 80:18 So will not we go back from thee: quicken us, and we will call upon thy name.

Without Grace we cannot truly seek him. Revival will stir our hearts to seek him!

We cannot come out of bondage without revival!

> Ezra 9:8, 9 And now for a little space grace hath been *shewed* from the LORD our God, to leave us a remnant to escape, and to give us a nail in his holy place, that our God may lighten our eyes, and give us a little reviving in our bondage. For we *were* bondmen; yet our God hath not forsaken us in our bondage, but hath extended mercy unto us in the sight of the kings of Persia, to give us a reviving, to set up the house of our God, and to repair the desolations thereof, and to give us a wall in Judah and in Jerusalem.

The Purpose of Revival

Chapter Ten
Redemption of the Times

I recently preached a message about redeeming the times. I thought much of it would be perfect here. The Lord has been speaking to me about this one phrase "Redeeming the Times." We're just going to begin reading in Ephesians 5:14. "Awake, you who sleep. Arise from the dead and Christ will give you light."

Awake-it's a call to an awakened. It's a call to revival, and revival simply means to live again. We need to wake up spiritually. Something happens when there is an awakening, we arise from the dead, and Christ will give you the light.

So the call is to awake, and that's what God is saying prophetically right now. Awake out of compromise. Awake out of religion and tradition. Awake to spiritual hunger. Awake to righteousness or a desire to have an encounter with God again. Awake us. "Wake us up, oh God. Wake us up Holy Spirit so that we can know what revival is." When I read the word awake, I started thinking about what it means to wake up.

The giant is the sleeping church.

God wants His church to wake up. God wants His giant to arise and take its place, but we've been lulled to sleep spiritually. Paul begins his message about redeeming the time. He begins the message with a call to revival, a call to awakening, a call to live again, a call to wake up out of compromise, and say I need an encounter. "Come Holy Spirit. I need to live again. I need the spirit of revival." Awake and Christ will give you light.

> Ephesians 5:15 See then that ye walk circumspectly, not as fools, but as wise,

The days are short. Therefore, do not be unwise, but understand what the will of the Lord is. Redeeming the time has to do with walking in the will and the purpose of God-understanding what the will and the purpose of God is.

Verse 18 says, "Do not be drunk with wine, but be filled the Spirit." So, right in the midst of this call to awaken in this message of redeeming the time, God says be filled with the Spirit. The key to revival and awakening is an encounter with the Holy Spirit-to constantly keep being filled with the Holy Spirit. I stopped and read that phrase again in Verse 16, redeeming the time, and I thought to myself, "How can we redeem time?"

The word redeeming means to buy back an opportunity that was lost. Redeeming the times means to be careful to take advantage of every opportunity that God gives us. I don't know about you, but I've had times of hopelessness, regret, and despair over opportunities that I know I had and missed. If I could have done it differently, I would have even went back in time and said, "Help me, Lord." This happens in our life this way many times. In addition, I was thinking how I could redeem time.

Redemption of the Times

"God, is it possible time that has been lost has been given back to me?" When I started thinking about redeeming the time, I realized that God was speaking to me about the power of redemption. Now when we talk about redemption, we use the word redeemed.

We go back to the moment that the blood of Jesus washed us and cleansed us. We remember the day when we came into salvation and were redeemed by the blood of the Lamb. Thank You, God for redemption. I remember the day when I was saved and born again.

The Lord was speaking to me about not just the cleansing and forgiveness through the blood, but that we've been redeemed. They've been singing in heaven, "We've been redeemed by the blood of the Lamb." I thought about what that means. I know what it means in the context of how the blood of Jesus has bought back, and I think about the free gift of salvation.

But the Lord was speaking about a whole lot more than just the gift of redemption that came in the moment of salvation. He was saying, "I want to redeem and buy back every opportunity that has been lost because you weren't careful to take advantage of the opportunity that was presented before you, because the days and the time are short. I need to add days or I need to accelerate time." I started thinking these thoughts and meditating on the phrase, redeeming the time.

Immediately I thought that even in the Lord, we could rewrite history. Not just redeeming the time and rewriting history, but redeeming the time has to do with acceleration, where God can do in six minutes what would take six years. Elijah had a supernatural season of acceleration and outran the chariots of Ahab. God can come upon me and cause me to do more in six minutes than six years, because a thousand years is as a day to the Lord.

The way that time works in the Spirit and the way that time works in eternity are so different. If God has to add days, God can add days. The most amazing thing is God caused the sun to stand still. There's still a day missing. God said, "I'm not done yet. I've got to stop the sun for Joshua, because there is something that I need to get done." This is the purpose of God. The Scripture says we can taste of the powers of the future age, and now we can even go into the future and taste time.

I was thinking about what Esther said, for such a time as this-a kairos time, redeeming the time, an accelerating time, tasting of the future, the Holy Spirit telling me things yet to come. Bringing what was reserved for another day, bringing it into my day, and being a forerunner.

Rewriting history and going back to the future, redeeming time has to do with the will of God. It has to do with the purpose of God, and this pastor told me an amazing story. She was from Albuquerque, and she said, "There was a moment in my daughter's life in school." Your parents drive you to school, and they drop you off. They say things in front of your friends, and it just becomes a mark on your heart, a mark on your soul.

In the end, God's restoration is really better than it was in the beginning. The message I have is the Lord told me that there was a fresh anointing coming on our eyes to see in the Book of Ruth, things about Ruth, which is a vital message for the church today, because Ruth was all about the beginning of the harvest. The whole setting for the story of Ruth in the Bible was the harvest. And because we, as a church, are moving into the harvest at the end of the age, there are things that we need to understand about that message.

My message isn't about Ruth, but there are a lot of things in the Spirit about redeeming the time and restoration that I want to say about Ruth. The Lord has been speaking to me about when He restores, it's always greater and better than it was in the first place. Now we know Ruth means friendship and commitment, and Ruth is a true picture of intimacy.

The story of Ruth begins with Ruth and Naomi and their families having to leave Judah because there was a famine in the land. And it's not just in the natural but even a spiritual famine, and they had to go into Moab.

Naomi loses her husband. Ruth loses her husband. All of Naomi's sons die, and they are living in the land of leftovers really. They're living in a time of famine. Naomi is bitter and broken; so much so that she says don't call me pleasant.

Don't call me Naomi anymore. Call me weeping, call me bitter, because I was full, but now I'm empty. I've come back broken. I've come back empty.

When I went out of Judah to Moab, I was full, and they called me pleasant. My name was Naomi. Now my name is bitter. Call me Mara. Call me empty. Call me living in the land of leftovers. Call me living in debt. And here I am with my daughter-in-law.

Here's Ruth. And they are coming back now from Moab, because they heard that the Lord is visiting Judah again. I just remember this one part of the story out of Ruth 1:11, and it was when Naomi says to Ruth, "You've been released from your commitment. Go back to your family. Go back to your land." Remember when it said Ruth clung to her, just that one phrase? We cling to Jesus-commitment.

Ruth really was a friend. I love the story because Naomi says, "Why do you love me? I have no more sons to give. Why come with me when you can go back to your family and your land? You know my other daughter-in-law did. Come on. Go with her.

You're released. I bless you." Ruth clings to her and says, "You have no more sons to give. I don't love you with motive. I don't love you because you have something to give me. I love you because I know friendship, and I love you because I know intimacy." It's love without expecting anything.

Naomi says, "What do you want me to give? I have no more sons. I have nothing to give you. I am no longer Naomi-pleasant, full, and overflowing. I'm now Naomi-bitter, empty, and broken. I have nothing to give." And that's when Ruth said, "I'll love you." Ruth means friendship-friendship with God and commitment. Here is the thing that Ruth lost. Just like you and me outside of the covenant, Ruth married into something that was greater than she was, because she had a right. She had an inheritance through her husband, on her husband's father's side, Naomi's husband. Do you know what his name means? Kingship-the right to be entitled to be king, to be in the royal family, which means a social family and money.

There are a lot of things about being the daughter-in-law. The father-in-law has the right to be king, and now I've married into something kingly and royal, and it became my destiny through my husband.

he died, Ruth lost her vision and her inheritance. Ruth lost her dream. She had no more ties or right in the natural through relatives to make any kind of a claim to kingship, and that's what she lost too.

When we get to the end, we know about Boaz, the kingsman and redeemer, one of the greatest stories of romance, love, friendship, commitment, intimacy, and restoration. Ruth is the story of expecting nothing in return.

They come back to Judah, and she said, "I'm going to love you even though you're empty, Naomi. I'm going to love you even though you're broken. I'm going to love you even though your name is bitter and weeping.

I'm going to love you and you're not full, and you're not pleasant. I cling to you and you have no more sons to give. And you have nothing to give me in return, because that's what love is. It expects nothing, and I am a true friend. We're coming out of the land of leftovers." They come back to Judah and Boaz comes. Where is Ruth? She's in the field with the inheritance of the poor and the stranger.

Redemption of the Times

The poor and the stranger were the ones who had a right to what was leftover in the harvest. You couldn't glean from the field. You had to wait until the harvesters and reapers were done, then the poor and the stranger could come out into the harvest and pick up the leftovers.

Here is Ruth and Naomi living in the land of the leftovers. From pleasant, full, favored, and kingship to empty, broken, bitter, weeping, and gleaning in the land of the leftovers, in the time of famine. Then comes Boaz.

When Boaz came, he said, "Who is this woman? Tell her to come into my field. This woman cannot only come into my field, but I'm going to give her my field. I'm going to give her the best of my field. I'm going to give her the harvest, and she can reap with the reapers." And do you remember what Ruth said? Ruth said, "Why have I found such favor? Boaz, why have I found such favor?" That's the goodness of God.

Have you ever said, "God, why do You love me? God, why do I receive Your goodness? God, why do I receive Your favor?" And here is Ruth saying to Boaz, "I don't understand why you're good to me, and there is nothing that I gave you, and I have favor.

Even with all of these other women that have rights, and all of these other reapers, I've got a place in which there is something in me that you loved, that was attractive, that you gave me favor."

Do you remember what Ruth said in the beginning when she said I'm going to cling to you Naomi?

Redemption of the Times

She said, "Urge me, I'm going to follow you, and wherever you go, wherever you lodge, that's where I'm going to lodge. Wherever you live and where you go, that's where I'm going to go."

It's like when Jesus said the Son of Man has no place to lay His head. Wherever You go, I will follow You Jesus. Wherever You live, wherever You lodge, that's where I'm going to lodge. I'm going after the cloud and I'm going after the glory."

Ruth said, "I'm going to leave my land, my mother, my brother, my family, all that has become familiar to me in my land, my people, my culture in Moab, and I'm going to go into an unfamiliar people and unfamiliar family, an unfamiliar culture with nothing to give in return.

You have no sons to give me, and I'm going to love you, and I'm going to follow you, and I'm going to cling to you and model what true commitment, friendship, and intimacy." And she finds favor and she says, "Boaz, why do I have favor?" And here is what Boaz says, "Because you said to Naomi you were willing to leave land, father, brother, culture, and people."

I thought of this because I said to Jesus I will take up my cross. I will deny myself. I will lose my life, and wherever You go, I will follow, and wherever You lodge, I will lodge. I will be a friend of God and committed to God even though there is nothing to give that You haven't given already. I will love You because You're worthy.

This is why Ruth finds favor.

Redemption of the Times

Then the most amazing thing happens. Naomi says at midnight when the man is sleeping, "I want you to go to the man's feet, and whatever he tells you at his feet, I want you to do that."

I mean, what a prophetic message. I want you to go to his feet, and I want you to sit at his feet, and whatever he says at his feet, I want you to do that. Boaz wakes up and says, "There is a woman laying at my feet. Why are you laying at my feet?" And what a picture, like Mary sitting at the feet of Jesus.

Boaz wakes up, and he finds Ruth at his feet. The story goes on when redemption comes and Boaz comes. He not only buys back and assumes all of the debt of Ruth, but he buys back and assumes all of the debt of Naomi too. There was something in the favor that was on Ruth that brought the breakthrough and the restoration for the rest of her family.

There is something about when the jubilee comes. It's not only the liberty in the jubilee and the celebration of joy for you, but like Ruth, "I'm going to buy back and assume all of the debt that Naomi has too, and I'm going to bless you, and I'm going to bless Ruth though she has nothing to give me, but she has favor, because she's laying at my feet."

In the end, Ruth is released from debt and blessed. Naomi is released from debt and blessed. She's no longer called the woman that is bitter and Mara. She's now called the woman that's most blessed, and she's so blessed that when Ruth has a child, they said it's better than seven sons.

Redemption of the Times

This is what the Lord is releasing in this moment-in this hour. He's releasing and speaking about redeeming the time. Let me tell you what redeeming the time means.

In the Greek, redeeming means we can buy up ransom or rescue from loss all of those times in our life that we missed the will of God.

We, as believers, cannot only be forgiven of our pasts, but we can even travel back in time with God and see Him as a very present help in times past, present, and future. We can redeem those times from the past the enemy wanted to use for evil. Redeeming the time has to do with buying back every lost opportunity that we had, to ransom, and to rescue from lost.

Now I don't know about you, but I've had times where I've said the blood of Jesus will forgive me. The blood of Jesus will cleanse me. God has forgiven me, but the fruit of my sin is the mess that I made. It's like when you've made your bed, we've been taught, to lie in it. There is a consequence to sin.

There is this whole idea that when we mess up, there is forgiveness and cleansing, but somehow the consequence, discipline, and the fruit of our actions is forever the way that it has to be. God's forgiven me and I'm cleansed, but because of the choices that I've made, this is the way that it is in my marriage, in my business, in my church, or in my ministry.

People don't understand that we have been redeemed by the blood of the Lamb.

Not just in the moment of salvation, but the ongoing power of redemption that God is redeeming lost time, God is redeeming lost opportunity, so that God is ransoming, rescuing, and buying back the bondage that you came into. The Scripture says do not give place or inroads, nor give opportunity to the devil. We tend to think about the bondage, the oppression, the sickness, and the poverty that comes.

God forgave me and cleansed me, but this is the consequence of my sin. We don't understand that not only does God want to forgive and cleanse, but God wants to redeem us back from the bondage, sickness, and poverty that came because of our willful disobedience.

It is not just something that happened at the moment of the cross, but every day there's an opportunity to redeem an opportunity that was lost.

In Revelation 12:11, it says that we have overcome by the blood of the Lamb and the word of our testimony, and we did not love our lives to the point of death.

> Revelations 12:11 And they overcame him by the blood of the Lamb, and by the word of their testimony; and they loved not their lives unto the death.

So how do we use the blood of Jesus as a weapon of warfare? People talk about the blood of Jesus as a spiritual weapon.

I believe gone are the days in the 1970s where people were running around and sprinkling and pleading the blood of Jesus. God moves in faith. Hallelujah.

Faith comes when we honor and speak of the blood, but I don't really go around in the name of Jesus and say over demons, "I plead the blood over you." I believe there is another way. I wrote down five thoughts about understanding the blood and how it works, and how we can even use the blood of Jesus as a weapon of warfare.

We need to understand that the only basis that we have that's legal for the promises of God is the blood of Jesus. We understand the cross and what it's done.

We overcome by the blood of the Lamb. The only reason that I have victory is because of the blood and what the cross has already done. We testify, speak, and declare the power of what the blood has already done.

We want the devil to hear that we know what the blood has done. We testify of its power. We understand that who we are is because of what the blood has done, the righteousness of God. We have faith and trust in the blood's power.

The last key to overcoming is we love not our lives, and are dependent on the Holy Spirit to the point where we are willing to die to ourselves, deny ourselves, and lose ourselves, which becomes a great weapon of warfare.

The Lord spoke to me out of Isaiah 43:25. God just doesn't forgive and cleanse my sins, but we read, "I am He.

I am He who blots out your transgressions for My own sake, and I will not remember your sins. Put Me in remembrance. Let us contend together. Come to My Court." It's like the Heavenly Court. Let us contend together.

What are we contending over? The sin, debt, sickness, poverty, and disease that's the fruit of sin. It's one thing to be forgiven and cleansed, but it's the circumstance. There is still the fruit. There are still the consequences of sin. There's still the bondage.

There are still the areas of your life where you've lost peace and joy, and there is grief and sorrow because of the fruit and the decisions that you made. You know that God has forgiven you, but you're still walking in consequence. God is saying, "Let's contend together where the devil believes he has legal basis, and that he is the accuser."

It is only in the blood of Jesus that we have legal basis to the promises of God, and God is saying, "Come to My court and contend with Me that you might be acquitted as if it never happened.

Declared righteous and justified. I want you to contend with Me so that you might be acquitted." If you're acquitted for your sin, it's as if it never happened.

God orders back all of the stuff that the devil took because of the door that you opened and the choice that you made when you sinned. Then God redeems that.

We want to understand what it really means to be restored. God said, "I will restore the wasted years that the locusts have eaten." When we're talking about redeeming the time, we're talking about the wasted years.

Redemption of the Times

If I could have been on fire and got a hold of the revelation that I have today when I was twenty, and if I could have made a different decision in my ministry, in my relationships, or if I could have made a decision when I was sixteen or when I was thirty, I would not have to live with all of this regret.

When you're talking about redeeming time, you need to understand what time means. What time means is taking advantage of every opportunity and occasion to do good. How many times do you believe that we have failed opportunities that we had to do good?

However, God can rescue and buy back, and bring us back to the crossroad. Forty years they went around the same mountain. God said forty days and they went around. He said after the first time, "This is a forty day journey, Israel. You made it forty years." God so wanted them to get it right that He just kept bringing them opportunity, and opportunity, and opportunity for forty years.

Every opportunity that you've lost, God will give it back, redeem the time, and ransom back the bondage you came into because of the decision that you made after you became saved.

You put yourself back under the law of sin and death in choices that you've made.

Redeeming the time has to do with understanding kairos, and I want you to understand the concept of kairos which means time, the idea of time. It's not about minutes and seconds, wristwatches and sandals. It's about the flow of time, a specific measurement of time, kairos time. Kairos carries with it the idea of the right time, predetermined time, and opportune time.

How much time before lunch would not be the word kairos. It is time to have lunch would be. It's time. It's time, praise God. One is speaking of time in minutes and seconds, where the other one is speaking of a point in time.

A point of determined time-predestined time in eternity a thousand years is as a day, the flow of time. I want you to think about the flow of time.

Examples of kairos is the time where you had better get moving, praise God. The crops aren't going to harvest themselves. Kairos is the appointed time, the proper time, and the slice of time where we have opportunity. Eventually though, the kairos divine opportunity time will slip away, and that's why Paul said to be careful, the days are evil.

We can't even begin to buy back the power of the time that we lost already until we understand to get it back from the enemy. We need to awake first. We need an awakening.

Redeeming the time is the idea that we purchase out of slavery the fleeting opportunities that we were presented with. In other words, make the most out of every opportunity. Make the most of your time. Stepping out of the kairos moment of God's time is referring to the will of God, the purpose of God.

This is how we tend to look at time. In every moment of life, family, relationships, and business-we blow it all of the time. With the idea of redeeming the time, God is saying not only am I cleansing and forgiving, but also I'm going to acquit.

You're acquitted. "I want you to understand that I not only forgive, I block out your transgressions." It's as if it never happened. So that means the consequence of your sin never happened either.

That means it's not restoration until the consequence and the fruit of the action that you made is redeemed too. It isn't restoration until I'm back preaching in stadiums. It isn't restoration. God brings back a lost opportunity.

In God, the flow of time never stops moving. At any juncture you get off of the road, and when you receive the power of redemption, redeeming the time, not just forgiveness and cleaning, but redeeming the time, you get to step back into the will and purpose of God, the constant flow of time, as if you never got out in the first place.

You don't start all over again, you step right back in the same juncture and keep going on. If you get off again and you fall into some willful compromise and religion, and you're not praying, then all of a sudden you decide to say, "God forgive me."

Then you begin to seek the will of God, and your passion becomes doing the will of God again. Even after all of these years, you're like can I come back?

There was a gift of healing, and power, and miracles, and all of these years later, you come back. You get to step right back in, and the time keeps moving. It never stopped moving.

Redemption of the Times

You don't have to make penance, because the way time works in heaven doesn't work by days, calendars, minutes, seconds, and wristwatches.

It's one constant flow of time-the beginning, the first and the last, the Alpha and the Omega. The beginning is in the end, the end is in the beginning. At any moment, God can bend time to make it fit what you are doing and put you into time so that it's as if you've never lost time.

I will restore to you the wasted years that the locusts have eaten and I will make it so perfect that it will be as if you were never divorced. It'll be as if you never went bankrupt.

It'll be as if you never sinned, and I can rewrite history and even replace memory. I can make you whole and perfect. Not only do I forgive, but also I blot out your transgression as if it never happened.

So now the devil can't stand before the throne and say, "Yeah, you're forgiven, but the consequence of that action..." God would say, "Contend with Me, and you will be acquitted, because it's so perfect being in the blood of Jesus."

You are coming into Ruth, and God is going to give the inheritance back and your kingsman Redeemer comes, and you're moving out of the land of leftovers, and you're moving out of the land of weeping and bitter, and you're coming into the land of fullness and abundance.

Naomi is going to be pleasant again. God will assume your debt, praise God. He will assume your mortgage, praise God. He will buy back your land, your house, and your property.

Redemption of the Times

How many of you know that's jubilee? When it happens to you and me, anybody and everybody that has ever blessed us and helped us has to be restored too.

God, in Ruth's restoration, brought restoration to Naomi. In God's restoration to you, your whole family and anybody that has been affected by decisions you made, have to come back in the blessing too. That's what redemption is.

Grab hold of this message today friends, and receive all the Lord has for you now.

Redemption of the Times

Chapter Eleven
Full Pentecost

We read in the Bible like it's a story book of Pentecost. If we are believers we must believe that it did in fact happen. Also we must believe that the selfsame experience can take place today. This is the word and passion in my spirit in recent weeks that God would reignite the flame of the Holy Spirit and Pentecost that is in us!

Imagine- we have the original FIRE and POWER that fell on the day of Pentecost. What an amazing thought that the same Spirit burning in and through Peter and Paul also burns in me. My original DNA, link, and nature is made up of the fire that fell on that day. Many of us simply need God to stir it up again so it burns in us in a new and powerful way. Even as I write about it, I hunger for more and feel a fresh Spirit of revival for the church in America. This chorus by Bethel Music and Brian Johnson captures the true Spirit of our need for His fire today.

I'm laying down my life I'm giving up control I'm never looking back I surrender all I'm living for Your glory on the earth

Full Pentecost

This passion in my heart This stirring in my soul To see the nations bow For all the world to know I'm living for Your glory on the earth

For the sake of the world burn like a fire in me! Light a flame in my soul for every eye to see! For the sake of the world burn like a fire in me!

We need a fresh experience (revival) of the original Pentecost experience that we received when we were born again and filled with the Spirit. We need the same fire from the 2,000-year-old Pentecost that the disciples and early church received. It burns in us still and needs to be ablaze again like an unquenchable, contagious flame. We need to believe God that His outpouring on "all flesh" will manifest itself in its fullness again. We no longer have to just talk about the Day of Pentecost or about the Azusa Street Revival. There are some things that God is releasing fresh now and He is pouring out His Spirit on the church.

When I talk about a "full Pentecost," I'm not just talking about power, revival, harvest, signs, and wonders. I'm talking about visions, dreams, prophecy, encounters, heavenly signs above, and wonders beneath. We need to believe God for all the signs of a full Pentecost again.

We need a new fresh outpouring like in the days of Evangelist Maria Woodworth-Etter! They say in her meetings people had regular open visions and even sometimes hundreds at a time were slain in trances like dead men. They described detailed visions of Jesus, angels, hell, and heaven after being in the revival atmosphere. I want an outpouring of power and an outpouring of fresh, supernatural encounters with heaven.

I'm not preaching a denomination or organization, but a hunger for a fresh experience with the fire that comes by the Spirit of God. We need to have a fresh encounter with the Holy Spirit that will look like Pentecost in fullness again!

One truth God is really restoring to the church again is visions, revelation, prophecy, and dreams with confirming heavenly signs and wonders. It's amazing that many Pentecostals accept a baptism in the Spirit with tongue talking, harvest, signs, healings, and wonders. But when it comes to heavenly dreams, prophecy, encounters, and visions, we stop short! Many of us love the idea of Pentecost but we are lacking the full experience, which includes supernatural encounters and experiences.

We are contending for a fresh outpouring of the Spirit and glory of God. We are asking for a full Pentecost complete with supernatural encounters and power to spread the fire of revival and healing. Let's ask God to ignite in us a fresh fire that's so hot it cannot be stopped. As John Wesley once said "Set yourself on fire and let the world watch you burn."

Full Pentecost

Chapter Twelve
Position to Receive

I believe as far as people in America and even around the world the key to finding God is in the quiet place. How can we hear unless we listen. The Bible says that Mary sat at Jesus' feet. Do you know what Mary was doing? She was listening. Because she positioned herself in a place of surrender and quietness, she learned to hear His voice. I can just picture her looking on the Lord's face and thinking: Oh, You're awesome. You're so wonderful! She sat gazing into His eyes and listening to His voice. Soaking is also about positioning ourselves in prayer at Jesus' feet as Mary did. I want to reposition you in your prayer time. Do you know Mary's position—that position of quietness and yielding? Are you touching intimacy with Jesus, or are you more like Martha with her "to do" list?

I often tell the Lord, "Your presence is good enough. I just want to be with You. I don't want to talk to You about my cares or my needs. You know the things I have need of anyway." Jesus said, "Your Heavenly Father knows that you need all these things (Matt 6:30). If you can grasp this truth your needs will be met more frequently and won't be dependent on your asking. Yes, one aspect of our relationship with God involves asking. But God wants to bring us to a new level of relationship that of lovers. In the natural, lovers often want to do things to bless their beloved, whether they're asked to or not. God wants to draw us into this same intimacy.

Sometimes all I do is sit at His feet and bask. That's it. Almost every teaching and revelation found on my audio and book table has come out of those soaking times. God has dropped revelation on me so fast that sometimes I've written four sermons at once. It had nothing to do with me; God would just burn the revelation inside me. Oh that's where God wants to bring us! God is calling the church back to intimacy and friendship with Him. What does the Bible say God wants of us? "He has shown you, O man what is good; and what does the Lord require of you...to walk humbly with your God." (Mic. 6:8). O, how the Father longs for you to walk with Him, to enjoy fellowship with Him. The Father longs for your presence more thank you long for His.

- Read the Word quickly and aloud so you hear it.
- Respond to it with your heart and mind. Respond to the passages that were most meaningful and reread those.
- Recollect or meditate with an open mind and heart to god's will.
- Rest in His presence.

Following are some powerful scriptures to kick-start your meditation and motivate you to continue with this life-changing way of connecting with God and His Word:

Psalms 119:10 With my whole heart have I sought thee: O let me not wander from thy commandments.

Position to Receive

Colossians 3:16 Let the word of Christ dwell in you richly in all wisdom; teaching and admonishing one another in psalms and hymns and spiritual songs, singing with grace in your hearts to the Lord.

Proverbs 4:20 My son, attend to my words; incline thine ear unto my sayings.

Proverbs 4:22 For they *are* life unto those that find them, and health to all their flesh.

Deuteronomy 11:18-21 Therefore shall ye lay up these my words in your heart and in your soul, and bind them for a sign upon your hand, that they may be as frontlets between your eyes. And ye shall teach them your children, speaking of them when thou sittest in thine house, and when thou walkest by the way, when thou liest down, and when thou risest up. And thou shalt write them upon the door posts of thine house, and upon thy gates: That your days may be multiplied, and the days of your children, in the land which the LORD sware unto your fathers to give them, as the days of heaven upon the earth.

Position to Receive

Chapter Thirteen
The El Shaddai Blessing!

We must be Sons of God that knows our God as all sufficient. In recent days, the Lord has really been stirring me about His promise that He is "The All Sufficient One" Almighty God. As I was praying in Salzburg, Austria in my hotel room, the Lord impressed on me that He wanted to come to us with a visitation as El Shaddai with His blessing. During this encounter with the Lord, the Holy Spirit spoke to me about "more than enough"-this is a time of overflow. There is an impartation in this teaching that will lead you into the breakthrough you are praying for. As you read this new article, may you receive the blessings of El Shaddai. "May El Shaddai bless you, make you fertile and numerous" (Genesis 28:3).

God wants to do more than just meet and sustain my needs-He wants to come in super abundance and overflow. The visitation Abraham had is twofold in purpose. God will sustain-He is omnipotent and He will be super-abundant (nourishing) in nature. The Hebrew name for "Almighty God" is "El Shaddai"-the name in which God first revealed Himself to Abram.

"And when Abram was ninety years old and nine, the LORD appeared to Abram, and said unto him, I am the Almighty God; walk before me, and be thou perfect. "And I

The El Shaddai Blessing!

will make my covenant between me and thee, and will multiply thee exceedingly" (Genesis 17:1-2 KJV).

Here, El Shaddai implies more than just Almighty God-as powerful, strong mountain, fortress, conquering one-but also the one who gives strength, grace, and power in man's weakness and frailty to endure. It is a promise that He will multiply us exceedingly and make us fruitful. El Shaddai is also said to refer to the nature of God that determines exactly what is enough for each of us: how much blessing a person needs or how much suffering a person can endure.

God revealed Himself as God Almighty when Abraham was struggling to believe that God could still carry out His promise to make him a father of many nations. God's name in this context conveys His ability to fulfill His promises. Of course, Abraham was weak in his body being 99 years old, but after all those years of believing for the promise of a son, there was opportunity for Abram to grow weak in faith, but he didn't! I believe one of the key reasons to Abraham's strength in believing faith was this visitation of Almighty God. It was like God was coming as El Shaddai with His blessing to impart, sustain, and bless Abraham so he could see the promise fulfilled.

God reveals Himself as Almighty God (El Shaddai) in those moments of our greatest weakness and temptation to give up. He comes to confirm His promise to us and give us supernatural strength that we need to continue in faith until the promise is fully manifest.

Theologian A.W. Pink in Gleanings in Genesis says, "The revelation which God here made of Himself was well suited to the occasion. This was the first time that He revealed Himself as 'the Almighty.' None but One who possessed all power could meet Abram's need at this time. Ninety and nine years of age, his body dead; Sarah barren and long past the age of childbearing-how could they have hope to have a son? But with God all things are possible. And why? Because He is El Shaddai, the All-Sufficient One." He has come to meet our need in fullness.

Charles Spurgeon spoke of El Shaddai this way, "Here is this name, 'El Shaddai;' 'El,' that is, 'the strong one,' for infinite power dwells in Jehovah. How readily may we who are weak become mighty if we draw upon Him! And then, 'Shaddai,' that is to say, 'the unchangeable, the Invincible.' What a God we have then, who knows no variableness, neither shadow of turning, against whom none can stand! 'El,' strong; 'Shaddai,' unchangeable in His strength; always therefore strong in every time of need, ready to defend His people."

The original promise God gave to Abram in Genesis 12:1-3 would not be fulfilled until the Lord visited him in Genesis 18:1-10. It took more than 25 years for the fulfillment of that promise. In this passage in Genesis 17:1-2, it was after 12 years of enduring faith and patience for the promise that God had already given him many years ago.

In fact in Genesis 17:1, this was already the sixth time that God had come to give Abraham the same promise and confirm the covenant that He made years earlier. It would be another 13 years before the angel of the Lord would come in Genesis 18:10 to announce the release of the full promise.

The El Shaddai Blessing!

Understanding this first visitation where God revealed Himself as Almighty God is important in this text. God's name in Scripture is intimately linked to His divine nature, character, and actions. It is important to study this Hebrew name for God to see the many things that God is not only saying to Abraham but also doing in him in this passage. As you come to truly know God as El Shaddai, God Almighty, you will be enabled to lay hold of His power and His sufficiency to carry out what He has promised. This is the visitation that gave them the faith here.

> Romans 4:19-21 And being not weak in faith, he considered not his own body now dead, when he was about an hundred years old, neither yet the deadness of Sara's womb: He staggered not at the promise of God through unbelief; but was strong in faith, giving glory to God; And being fully persuaded that, what he had promised, he was able also to perform.

> Hebrews 11:11 Through faith also Sara herself received strength to conceive seed, and was delivered of a child when she was past age, because she judged him faithful who had promised.

When we have a full revelation of the Hebrew meaning of the name Almighty God (El Shaddai), we can begin to understand what the El Shaddai blessing is.

Definition of Almighty God (El Shaddai): El comes from a root word meaning "might, strength, power, and strong one like a mountain." It means "The All Sufficient God or sustainer." It indicates that Shaddai is related to the word for breasts (shadaim), indicating sufficiency and nourishment. It occurs 48 times. It is God's complete sufficiency to nurture and nourish the fledgling nation into fruitfulness and abundance. Indeed, God first uses this name when He refers

The El Shaddai Blessing!

to multiplying (make fruitful) Abraham's offspring (Genesis 17:2).

As Abraham and Paul (and many other saints) learned, it is when we come to the end of ourselves and our own resources that we begin to "tap into" the sufficiency of the supply of El Shaddai and find that it is more than adequate for all our needs according to His riches in Christ Jesus.

Here's another great definition: "The God of Strength." Probably related to the word "mountain" and suggests the power or strength of God. This name also emphasizes God's covenant-keeping nature (Genesis 17:1). Some feel Shaddai is derived from a root that refers to a mother's breast, sustaining a newborn infant. If so, it conveys love, tenderness, and mercy-all that a mother is to a dependent newborn, so God is to His children.

The blessing of Almighty God is also directly linked to the blessing Jacob spoke over Joseph. Remember, Joseph means increase.

> Genesis 49:25, 26 *Even* by the God of thy father, who shall help thee; and by the Almighty, who shall bless thee with blessings of heaven above, blessings of the deep that lieth under, blessings of the breasts, and of the womb: The blessings of thy father have prevailed above the blessings of my progenitors unto the utmost bound of the everlasting hills: they shall be on the head of Joseph, and on the crown of the head of him that was separate from his brethren.

All of us have unfulfilled promises and many times face great discouragement, disappointment, and even grow weak in faith waiting for the fulfillment of what we know God promised. We have those moments in which we can grow weak and weary. This is when Almighty El Shaddai comes to give us the strength to endure and bless us with His over-abundant nature that nourishes us in faith and resources. He is the author and finisher of our faith. God initiates the promise and gives us grace so we can finish and see our faith and hope fulfilled.

"And God is able to make all grace abound toward you; that ye, always having all sufficiency in all things, may abound to every good work" (2 Corinthians 9:8 KJV). The purpose of His grace and all sufficient nature is that not only your needs be met, but that His abundance be released to you for the gospel.

So we see that the name El Shaddai speaks to us of God's power and sufficiency. It also speaks to us of the inexhaustible supply of God's riches and strength. It reminds us that His strength is made perfect in our weakness and His fullness in our emptiness.

Do we have needs that must be supplied? We must empty ourselves of our own pride and self-sufficiency and let El Shaddai fill us and make us fruitful. I believe God is bringing us into a season of divine fulfillment and sustaining us in faith. He is also blessing us with His strength and resources to meet our every need. I pray the El Shaddai blessing over you now in Jesus' name.

About the Author

Bill Vincent was a Pastor of a Church that moved in Healings, Miracles and the Prophetic. Bill Vincent is the Founder & President of Revival Waves of Glory Ministries although he is not a Pastor any longer, he still moves in the Prophetic, Healings & Miracles. The Ministry has regular meetings and travels to different cities to spread REVIVAL FIRE and the LORD'S MESSAGE. Bill has been in Ministry for many years and has led 3 successful Revivals in that time with tangible Healings & Miracles. He has flooded the market with Books that he has written and has published for other author's.

Recommended Books

By Bill Vincent

Overcoming Obstacles

Glory: Pursuing God's Presence

Defeating the Demonic Realm

Increasing Your Prophetic Gift

Increasing Your Anointing

Keys to Receiving Your Miracle

The Supernatural Realm

Waves of Revival

Increase of Revelation and Restoration

The Resurrection Power of God

Discerning Your Call of God

Apostolic Breakthrough

Glory: Increasing God's Presence

Love is Waiting – Don't Let Love Pass You By

The Healing Power of God

Glory: Expanding God's Presence

Receiving Personal Prophecy

Signs and Wonders

Signs and Wonders Revelations

Children Stories

Rapture Revelations

The Secret Place of God's Power

Building a Prototype Church

Breakthrough of Spiritual Strongholds

Glory: Revival Presence of God

Overcoming the Power of Lust

Glory: Kingdom Presence of God

Children Stories 10 Book Series

Faith Bible Adventures

Transitioning Into a Prototype Church

The Stronghold of Jezebel

Healing After Divorce

A Closer Relationship With God

Cover Up and Save Yourself

Desperate for God's Presence

The War for Spiritual Battles

Spiritual Leadership

Global Warning

There Are Millions of Churches

Destroying the Jezebel Spirit

Awakening of Miracles

Deception and Consequences Revealed

Are You a Follower of Christ

Don't Let the Enemy Steal from You!

A Godly Shaking

To Order:

Email:

rwgcontact@yahoo.com

Web Site:

www.revivalwavesofgloryministries.com

Mail Order:

Revival Waves of Glory

PO Box 596

Litchfield, IL 62056

Shipping $5.00

If you mail an order and pay by check, make check out to Revival Waves of Glory.

Most books are in multiple formats such as Hardcover, Soft-Cover, Ebook (such as Kindle & Nook), and Audio Books.

www.ingramcontent.com/pod-product-compliance
Lightning Source LLC
Chambersburg PA
CBHW072100290426
44110CB00014B/1758